The Moon

Carmel Reilly

This edition first published in 2012 in the United States of America by
Marshall Cavendish Benchmark
An imprint of Marshall Cavendish Corporation

Website: www.marshallcavendish.us

Other Marshall Cavendish Offices: Marshall Cavendish International (Asia) Private Limited, 1 New Industrial Road, Singapore 536196 • Marshall Cavendish International (Thailand) Co Ltd. 253 Asoke, 12th Flr, Sukhumvit 21 Road, Klongtoey Nua, Wattana, Bangkok 10110, Thailand • Marshall Cavendish (Malaysia) Sdn Bhd, Times Subang, Lot 46, Subang Hi-Tech Industrial Park, Batu Tiga, 40000 Shah Alam, Selangor Darul Ehsan, Malaysia

Library of Congress Cataloging-in-Publication Data

Reilly, Carmel, 1957-
The Moon / Carmel Reilly.
p. cm. — (Sky watching)
Includes index.
Summary: "Provides scientific information about the moon"—Provided by publisher.
ISBN 978-1-60870-581-8
1. Moon—Juvenile literature. 2. Astronomy—Observers' manuals—Juvenile literature. I. Title.
QB582.R534 2012
523.3—dc22
2010044016

Publisher: Carmel Heron
Commissioning Editor: Niki Horin
Managing Editor: Vanessa Lanaway
Project Editor: Tim Clarke
Editor: Paige Amor
Proofreader: Helena Newton
Designer: Polar Design
Page layout: Romy Pearse
Photo Researcher: Legendimages
Illustrator: Adrian Hogan
Production Controller: Vanessa Johnson

Printed in China

Acknowledgments
The author and publisher are grateful to the following for permission to reproduce copyright material:

Front cover photograph: Full moon shining over the ocean © Dreamstime/Tass.

Photographs courtesy of: Corbis, /Brooks Kraft, **24**, /Roger Ressmeyer, **14**; /YM YIK/epa, **26**; Dreamstime/Tass, **1**; Getty Images/Philip Nealey, **17** (left), /Roy Toft, **27**; Calvin J Hamilton/Solar Views, **11**; iStockphoto/pjmorley and NASA Earth Observatory, **7**, /Mike Sonnenberg, **5** (bottom), /Sergii Tsololo, border element throughout; NASA, **10**, **12**, **16**, **17** (right), **28**, /JPL/USGS, **13**, **15**, /Lunar and Planetary Laboratory, **5** (top and inset); Photolibrary/Science Photo Library, **29**, /Science Photo Library/Larry Landolfi, **8**, /Science Photo Library/NASA, **21**; Shutterstock/Sascha Gebhardt, **18**, /Hein Welman, **23**.

While every care has been taken to trace and acknowledge copyright, the publisher tenders their apologies for any accidental infringement where copyright has proved untraceable. They would be pleased to come to a suitable arrangement with the rightful owner in each case.

Please Note
At the time of printing, the Internet addresses appearing in this book were correct. Owing to the dynamic nature of the Internet, however, we cannot guarantee that all these addresses will remain correct.

Contents

Glossary Words

Words that are printed in **bold** are explained in the glossary on page 31.

What Does It Mean?

Words that are within a **box** are explained in the "What Does It Mean?" panel at the bottom of the page.

Sky Watching

When we sky watch, we look at everything above Earth. This includes what is in Earth's atmosphere and the objects we can see beyond it, in space.

Why Do We Sky Watch?

Sky watching helps us to understand more about Earth's place in space. Earth is our home. It is also a planet that is part of a space neighborhood called the **solar system**. When we sky watch we learn about Earth, and our neighbors inside and outside the solar system.

What Objects Are in the Sky?

There are thousands of objects in the sky above Earth. These are Earth's neighbors—the Sun, the Moon, planets, stars, and flying space rocks (**comets**, **asteroids**, and **meteoroids**). Some can be seen at night and others can be seen during the day. Although some are visible with the human eye, all objects must be viewed through a **telescope** to be seen more clearly.

When and How Can We See Objects in the Sky?

Object in the Sky	Visible with Only the Human Eye	Visible Only through a Telescope	Visible during the Day	Visible at Night
Earth's Atmosphere	✗	✗	✗	✗
Sun	✓ (Do not view directly)	✗ (View only with a special telescope)	✓	✗
Moon	✓	✗	Sometimes	✓
Planets	Sometimes	Sometimes	Sometimes	✓
Stars	Sometimes	Sometimes	✗	✓
Comets	Sometimes	Sometimes	✗	✓
Asteroids	Sometimes	Sometimes	✗	✓
Meteoroids	Sometimes	Sometimes	✗	✓

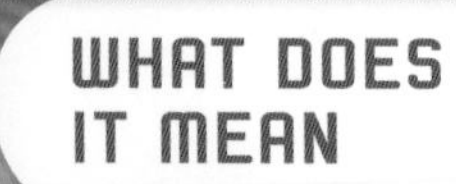

space The area in which the solar system, stars, and galaxies exist, also known as the universe.

The Moon

The Moon is a space object that can be seen in the sky without a telescope. It is visible on most nights, and sometimes during the day.

Moon Watching

People have always watched the Moon. However, it was only after telescopes were invented 500 years ago that **astronomers** could finally see its surface. Because of space exploration, we now know even more about the Moon. Today people now know what the Moon is made of, what conditions on the Moon are like, and how the Moon affects Earth.

Sky watching can be done during the day or night, with or without a telescope. Just look up!

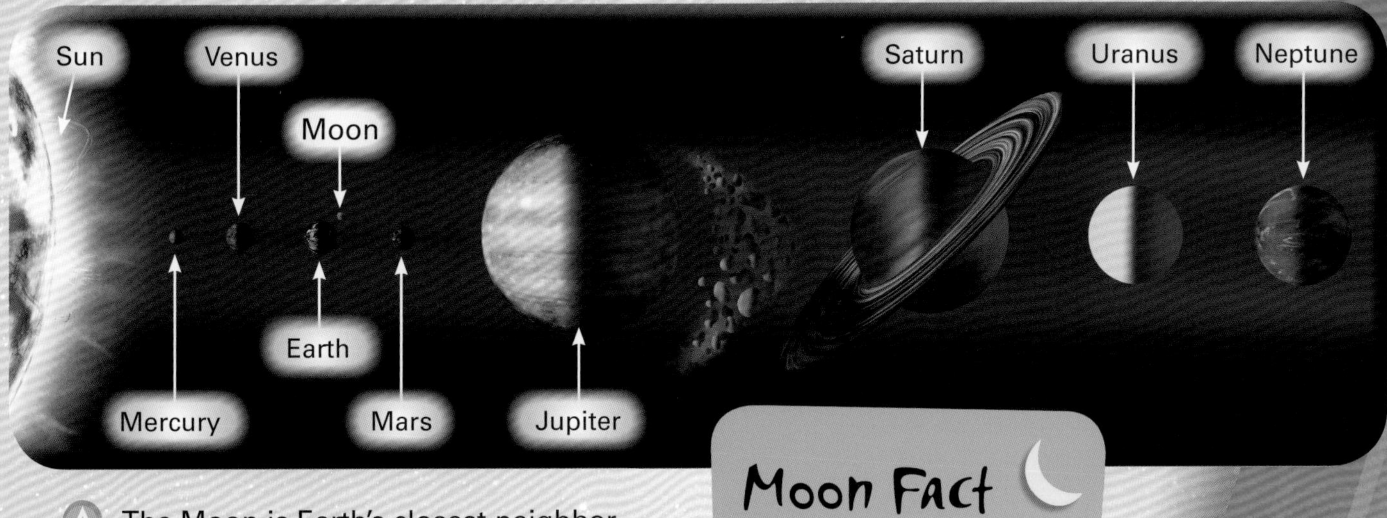

The Moon is Earth's closest neighbor in space. This diagram shows the approximate relative sizes of the Sun and the planets. The distances between them are not to scale.

Moon Fact

The fastest spaceflight from Earth to the Moon took 8 hours and 35 minutes. If you could drive there in a car, it would take 200 days to arrive!

What Is the Moon?

The Moon is a space object that **orbits**, or travels, around, Earth. It is a huge ball of rock, about one quarter the size of Earth. It first formed 4.5 billion years ago.

The Moon Is a Big Rock

Scientists believe the Moon formed from dust, rocks, and gas that were orbiting Earth. The Moon was hit by meteoroids and other space objects during its first years. About 3 billion years ago, volcanoes under the Moon's surface began to erupt. Hot **lava** burst from the volcanoes. About a billion years ago, the lava began to cool. The Moon became a ball of solid rock.

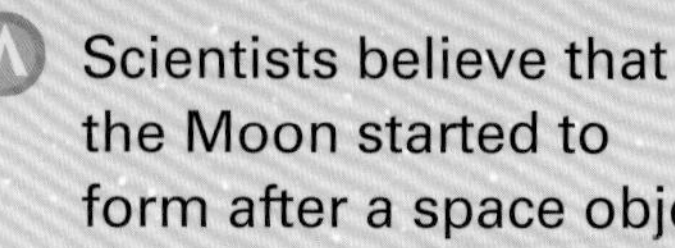

Scientists believe that the Moon started to form after a space object crashed into Earth.

WHAT DOES IT MEAN

orbits When one space object travels around another, larger space object.

The Moon Is a Satellite

The Moon is a **satellite** of Earth. Its orbit around Earth is slightly oval-shaped. This means that as it moves, the Moon's distance from Earth changes. At its closest, the Moon is 225,744 miles (363,300 kilometers) from Earth. At the farthest point of its orbit, it is 251,966 mi. (405,500 km) away from Earth.

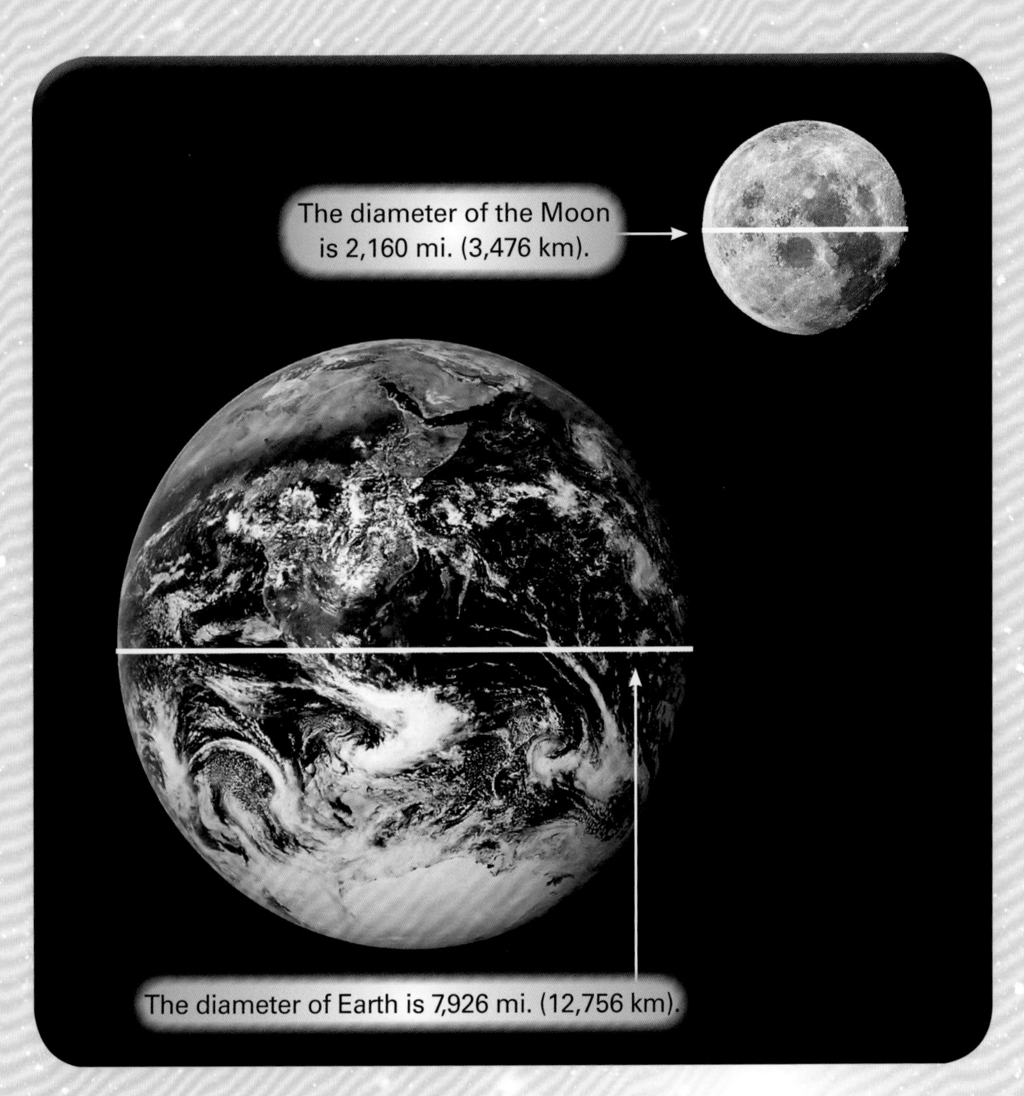

It takes 27.3 days for the Moon to orbit Earth and return to its starting point.

FAMOUS SKY WATCHERS

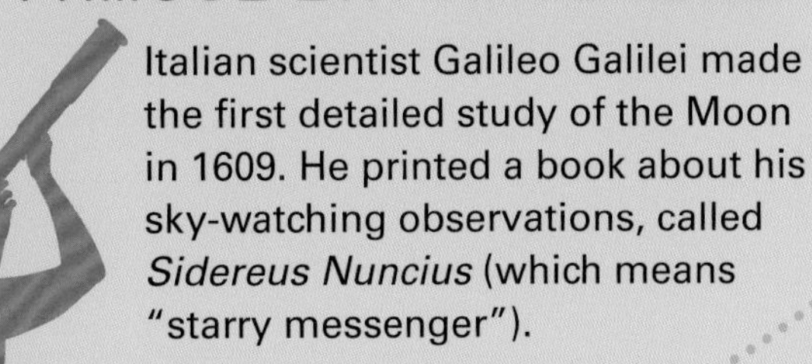

Italian scientist Galileo Galilei made the first detailed study of the Moon in 1609. He printed a book about his sky-watching observations, called *Sidereus Nuncius* (which means "starry messenger").

What Does the Moon Look Like from Earth?

The Moon is the largest and brightest object seen in the night sky. Dark markings are visible on its face. Its shape changes from night to night.

The Moon Has Dark Markings

Using telescopes, astronomers have discovered that the darker areas on the Moon's surface are **plains**. The lighter areas that can be seen are **highlands**.

It was not until the Moon was seen through a telescope that people were able to see what its surface was really like.

Moon Fact

From Earth the Moon seems to shine, but it does not produce its own light. The Moon's light is really a reflection of the Sun's light. The Moon reflects about 10 percent of the light that hits it.

The Moon Seems to Change Shape

Sometimes the Moon seems round, like a disc. At other times it appears to be a half circle or a crescent. These different shapes are called the **phases** of the Moon.

The Phases of the Moon

Half of the Moon is always lit by the Sun, while the other side is always dark. As the Moon orbits Earth, we only see the part of it that is lit by the Sun. When the Moon moves, different parts of it are lit, which makes it look as though it changes shape. It takes 29.5 days for the Moon pass through all of its phases.

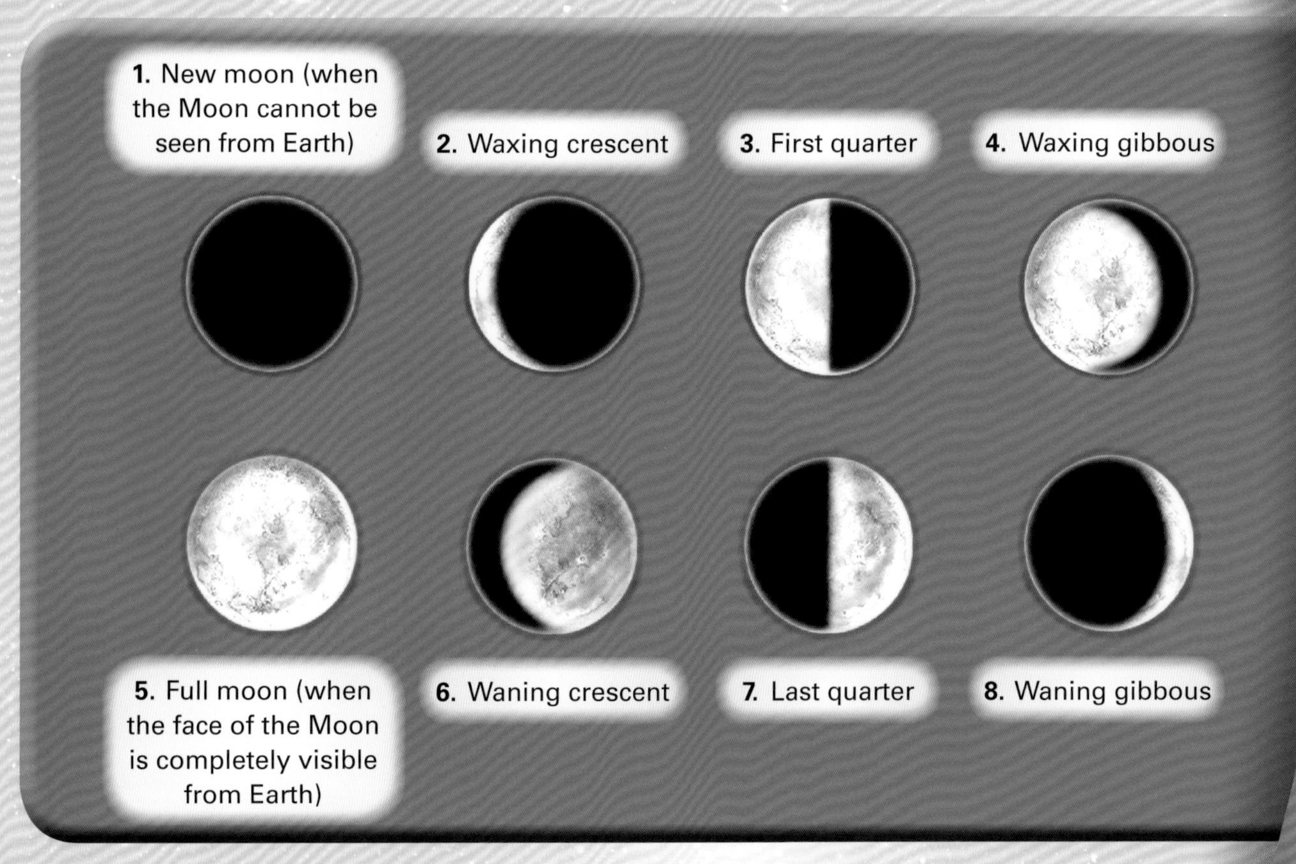

The phases of the Moon begin with a new moon and end with a waning gibbous.

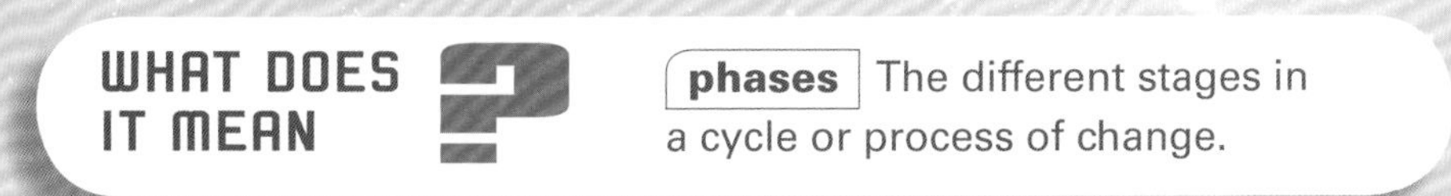

phases The different stages in a cycle or process of change.

What Is the Moon Made of?

From Earth we cannot tell what is inside the Moon. Scientists called lunar scientists gather information about the Moon from space exploration. They think the Moon has two layers of rock, called the crust and the mantle. These layers surround a small metal center, or core.

The Moon Has a Crust

The Moon's outside layer is called the crust. It is made from very hard rock. Samples taken by **astronauts** who have landed on the Moon help us understand what the Moon's crust is made of. These samples show that the crust contains mainly silicon, magnesium, iron, calcium, and aluminum.

The Moon's crust is made of very hard rocks that were formed when there were volcanoes on the Moon.

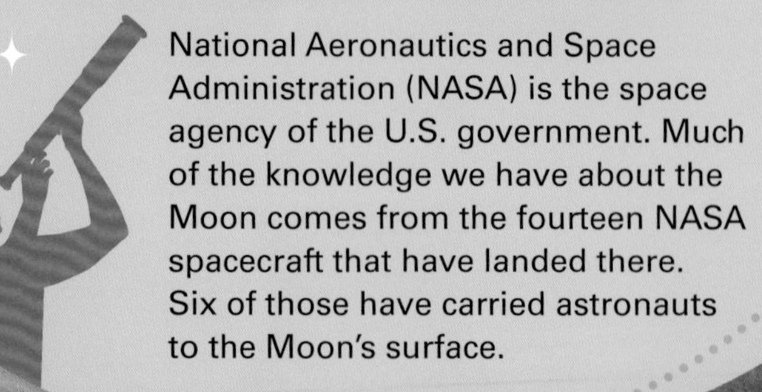

FAMOUS SKY WATCHERS

National Aeronautics and Space Administration (NASA) is the space agency of the U.S. government. Much of the knowledge we have about the Moon comes from the fourteen NASA spacecraft that have landed there. Six of those have carried astronauts to the Moon's surface.

The Moon Has a Mantle

Beneath the Moon's crust lies a thick middle layer, called the mantle. This is made up of two parts. The upper mantle, nearer the crust, is about 621 mi. (1,000 km) thick and is made of hard rock. The lower mantle is thought to be partly made up of **molten** rock.

The Moon Has a Core

Most scientists think the Moon has a small metal core, which is about 217 mi. (350 km) wide. This core is probably mainly solid, but its outer area may be molten metal.

Moon Fact

The Moon's crust is not the same thickness all over. It ranges from 66 to 394 feet (20–120 meters) in depth, and is thicker on the far side of the Moon than the near side.

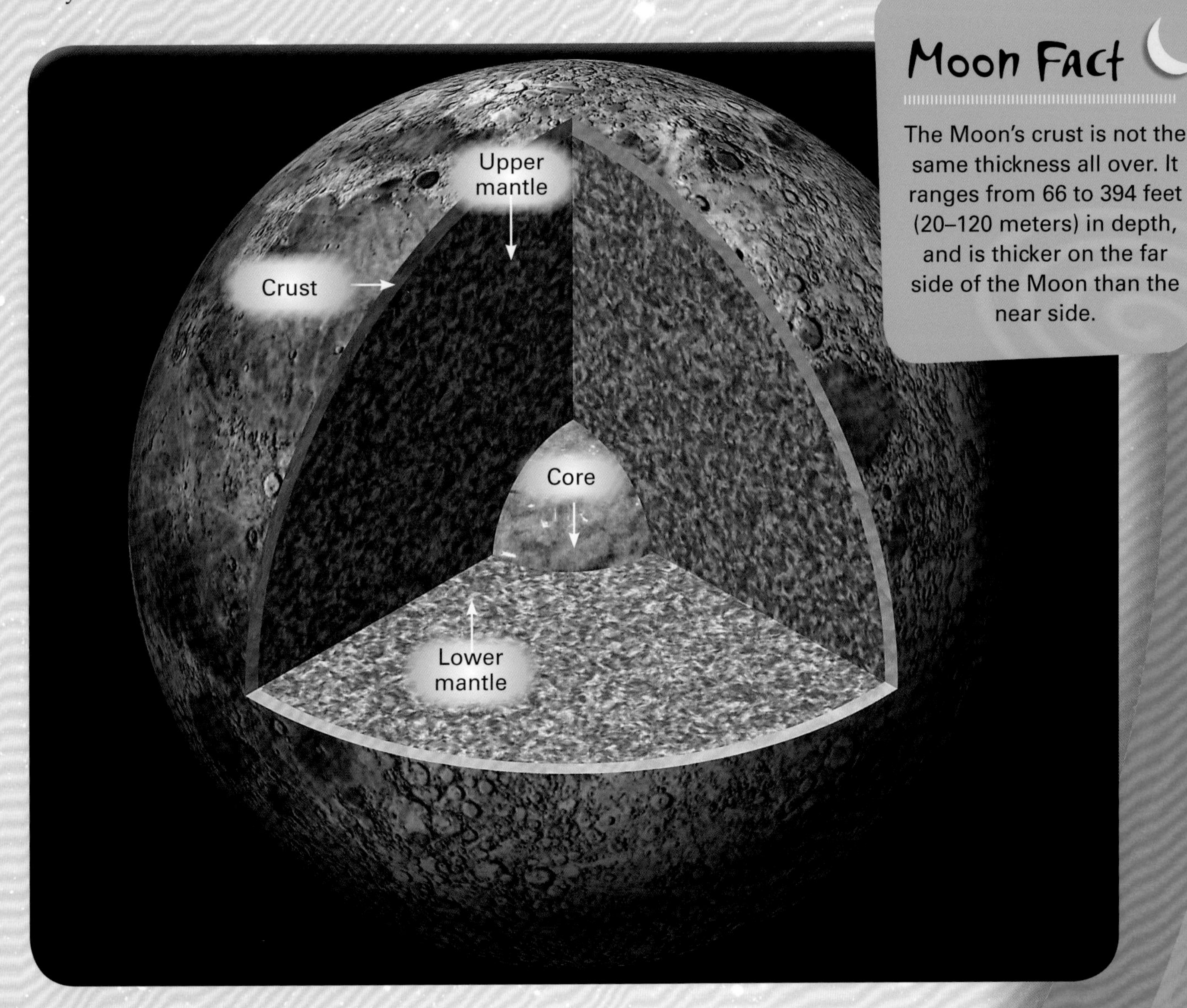

The Moon is made of mostly solid rock, but some parts near the center are probably liquid.

WHAT DOES IT MEAN?

molten Turned into a liquid form, or liquefied, by extreme heat.

What Is the Surface of the Moon Like?

From Earth, the Moon looks smooth, glowing, and white. But on the Moon's surface everything is rocky, dusty, and gray. Plains, highlands, mountains, and large holes called craters make up the Moon's landscape.

The Moon's Surface Is Rocky and Dusty

The surface of the Moon is covered in a layer of gray rock and dust called regolith. Regolith can be up to 66 feet (20 m) thick. It is formed when space objects, such as **meteorites**, crash into the Moon and smash the surface into small pieces of rock and dust.

The Moon's surface is made up of craters, low plains, highlands, and mountains. All of these are topped with a layer of rocks and dust.

Famous Sky Watchers

Astronaut Neil Armstrong was the first person to experience the Moon's surface. He walked on the Moon as part of the *Apollo 11* mission in July 1969.

Mountains are the highest areas.

Craters are large holes made by impacts from space objects.

Plains are low-lying areas.

Highlands are areas that are higher than plains.

The Moon's Surface Has Plains

Plains are large, low-lying, flat areas on the Moon's surface. From Earth we see them as dark areas on the Moon.

Plains Used To Be Craters

The plains on the Moon's surface were once craters. Billions of years ago, they were flooded with dark-colored lava that was pushed up to the surface by underground volcanoes. When the lava cooled it set into large plains.

Moon Fact

Early astronomers thought the dark areas on the Moon's surface were water. They called them by their Latin names: *mare*, meaning sea, and *oceanus*, meaning ocean.

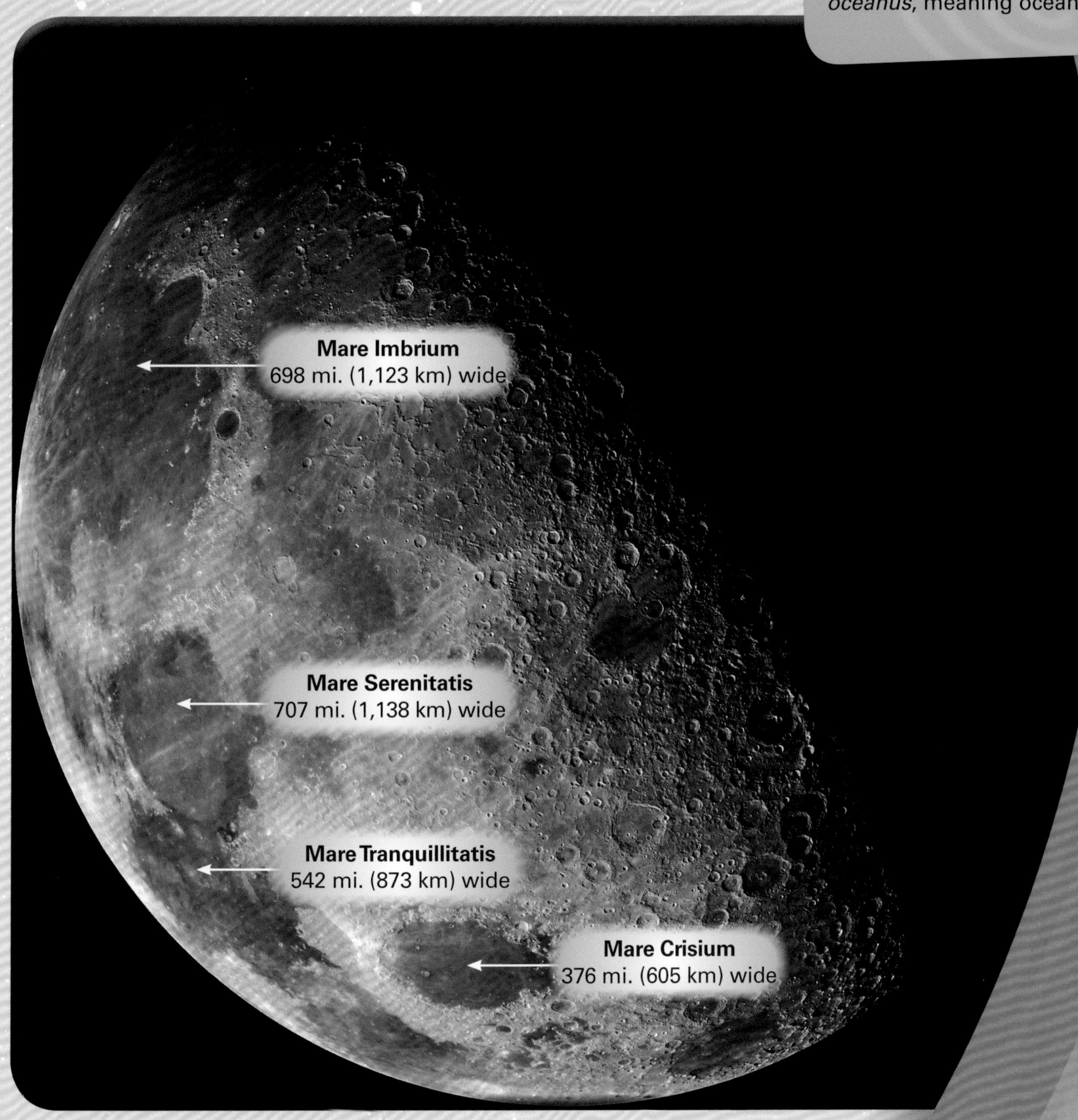

There are many plains, or seas, on the Moon.

The Moon's Surface Has Highlands

The highlands on the Moon are known by their Latin name, *terrae*, which means lands. They were given this name by early astronomers to set them apart from the "seas," or plains. From Earth, the highlands are visible as lighter-colored areas.

The Moon's Surface Has Mountains

Most of the mountains and mountain ranges on the Moon were formed after asteroid impacts. Mountains are usually found at the edges of deep craters or at the edges of plains. The largest mountain range on the Moon is the Apenninus mountain range.

The Apenninus mountain range runs for 373 mi. (600 km) along the edge of the Mare Imbrium. Its tallest peak is more than 1.9 mi. (3 km) high.

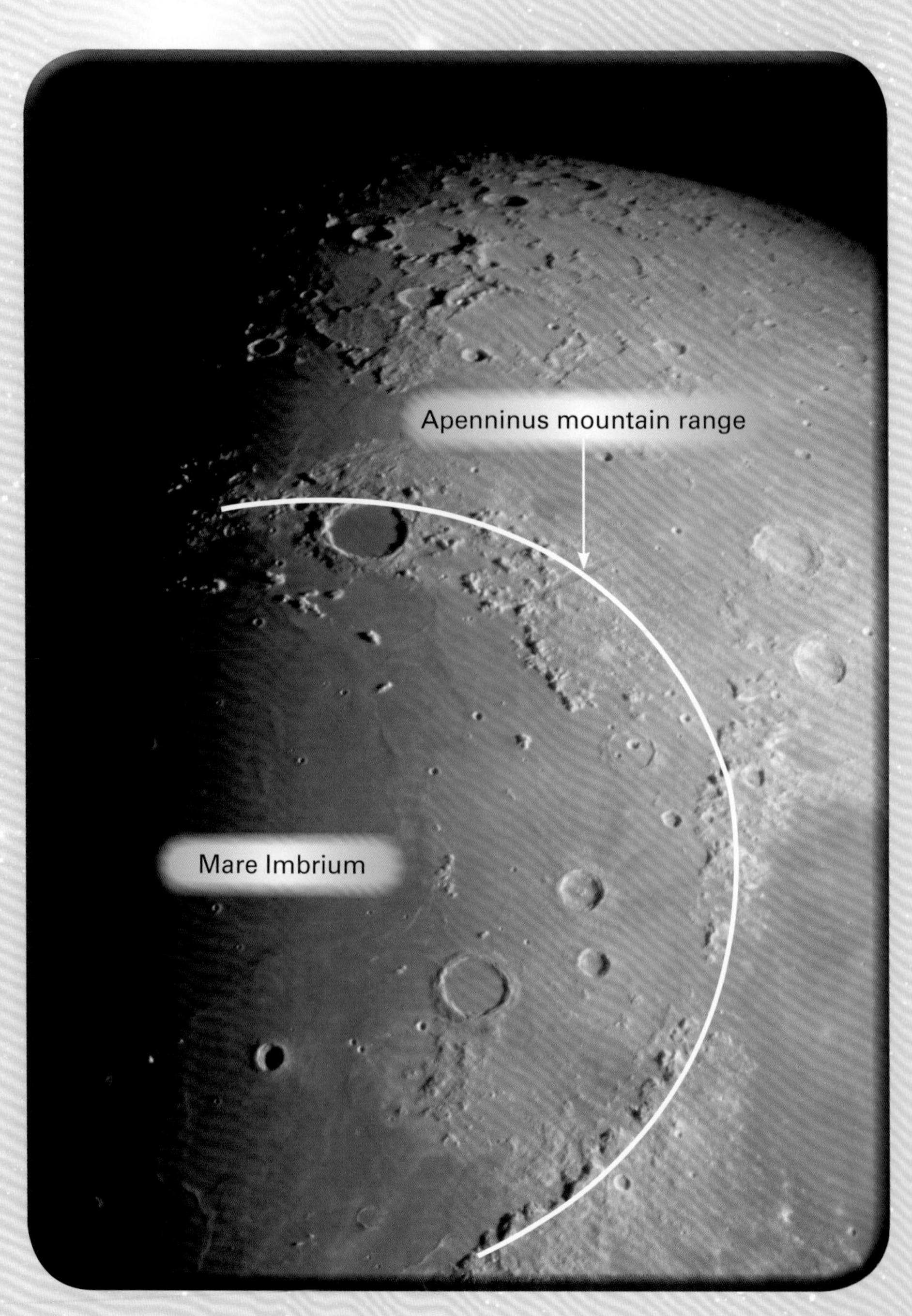

The Moon's Surface Has Craters

A crater is a large, bowl-shaped hole. The Moon's surface is covered in thousands of craters. Many of the Moon's craters are small, but some are very large. The South Pole–Aitken Basin is more than a thousand miles (1600 km) wide.

How Craters Were Formed

Some of the Moon's craters were formed by volcanoes. However, most were formed when asteroids and meteoroids hit the Moon's surface at high speed.

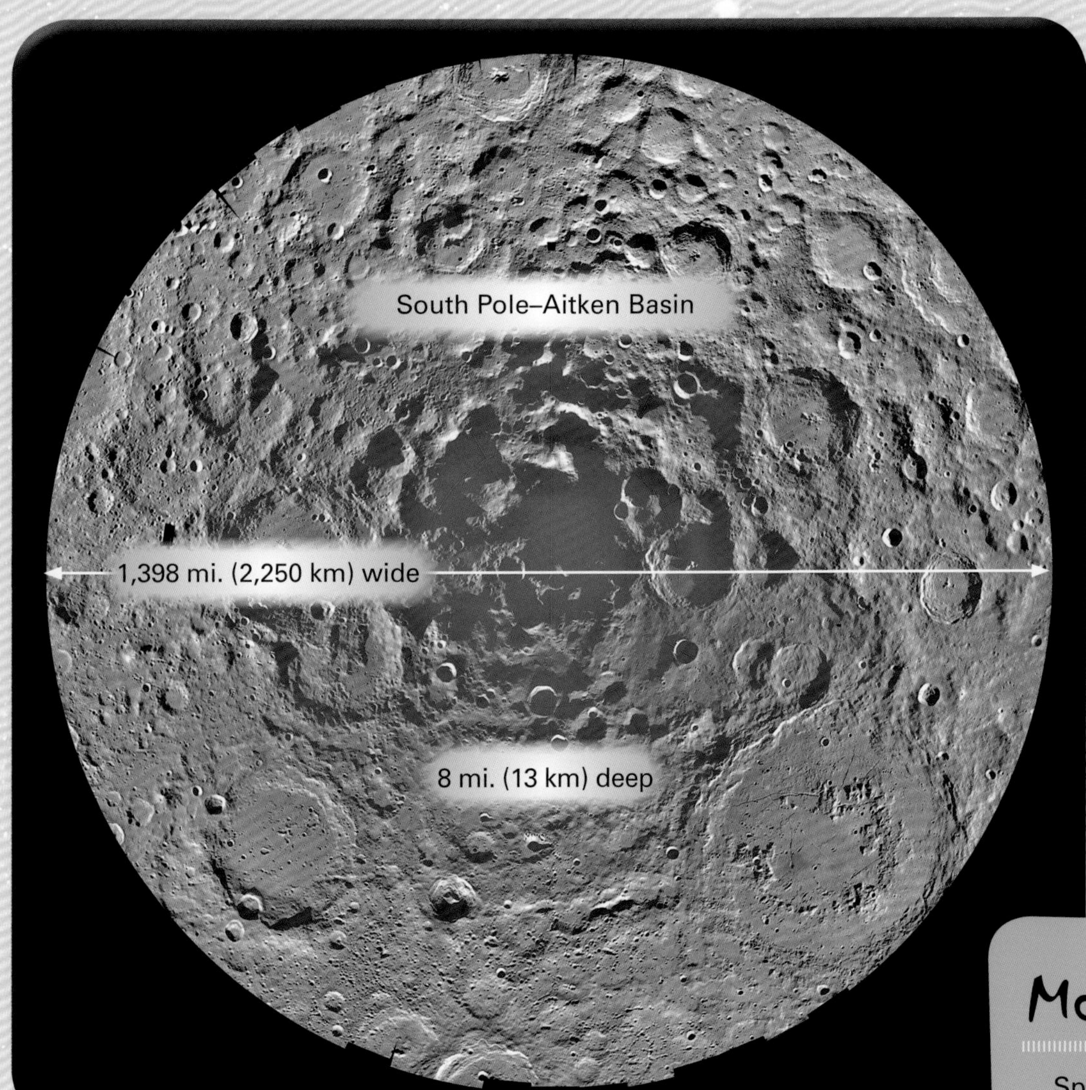

The Moon's surface is covered in craters. The largest is the South Pole–Aitken Basin.

Moon Fact

Space objects hit the Moon with incredible force. The craters that are formed by these impacts are usually about fifteen times bigger than the actual space object itself.

What Are Conditions Like on the Moon?

Conditions on the Moon are very different from those on Earth. Compared to Earth, there is less gravity. There is also no air or liquid water, **extreme** temperatures, no daylight, and no sound. Astronauts visiting the Moon need special equipment to survive.

The Moon Has Little Gravity

Gravity is a force that attracts all objects toward each other. The bigger an object, the stronger its **gravitational pull**. The Moon is a lot smaller than Earth. Earth's gravitational pull is six times that of the Moon.

V Everything on Earth weighs six times more than it would on the Moon. A person weighing 132 pounds (60 kilograms) on Earth weighs 22 lb (10 kg) on the Moon.

WHAT DOES IT MEAN ?

gravity The force that attracts all objects toward each other.

The Moon Has Little Atmosphere

Earth is surrounded by a layer of gases called the atmosphere. The atmosphere protects Earth from space objects, such as meteoroids, and helps to create conditions for life to exist. Compared to Earth, the Moon has little atmosphere because its weak gravity cannot hold gases close to its surface. Because of this, there is no air and only tiny amounts of ice on the Moon.

Moon Fact

Most meteoroids heading for Earth burn up in its atmosphere. Hundreds hit the Moon each year, as its atmosphere is not thick enough to stop them.

Earth's atmosphere provides water and air, so plant and animal life can exist. The Moon's thin atmosphere leaves it dry and airless.

The Moon Has Extreme Temperatures

Earth and the Moon are about the same distance from the Sun. Earth's dense atmosphere acts like a blanket to protect it from the Sun. This keeps its temperature even. The Moon does not have enough atmosphere to protect itself in the same way. This causes extreme temperatures.

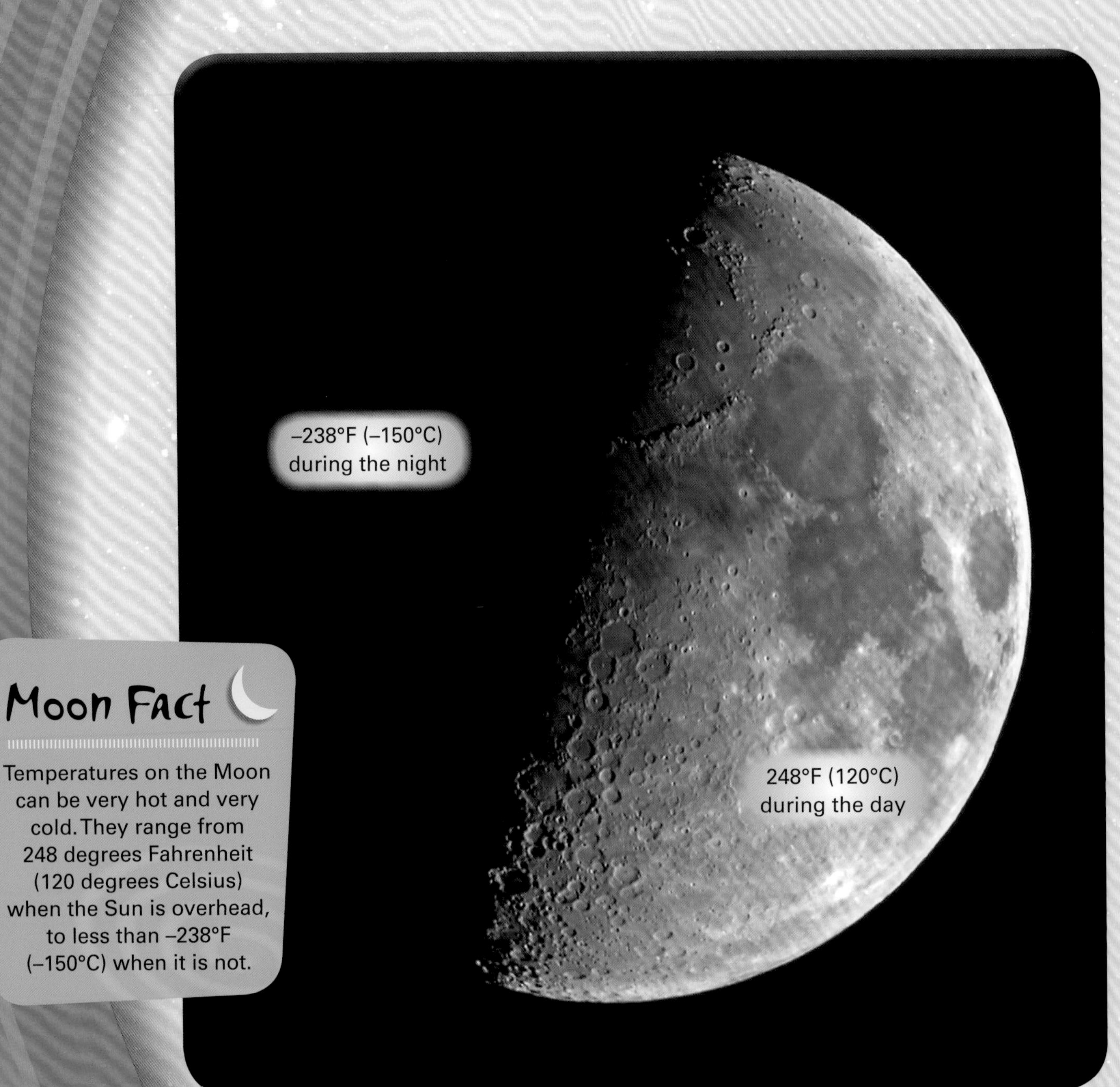

Moon Fact

Temperatures on the Moon can be very hot and very cold. They range from 248 degrees Fahrenheit (120 degrees Celsius) when the Sun is overhead, to less than –238°F (–150°C) when it is not.

The Moon's thin atmosphere cannot protect it from the Sun's heat during the day, or keep it warm at night.

The Moon Has No Daylight

There is no daylight on the Moon. The reason we see daylight on Earth is because our thicker atmosphere scatters the light from the Sun. Because the Moon's atmosphere is so thin, it does not scatter the light in the same way. Because of this, on the Moon the sky stays dark, even when the Sun is overhead.

There Is No Sound on the Moon

We hear sound on Earth because **sound waves** are carried through the atmosphere. On the Moon, there is not enough atmosphere to carry sound. When astronauts hammered a flagpole into the surface of the Moon during the Moon landing in 1969, it made no noise.

Ⓥ Astronauts visiting the Moon need special suits that allow them to breathe, and that protect them from extreme temperatures, and radiation.

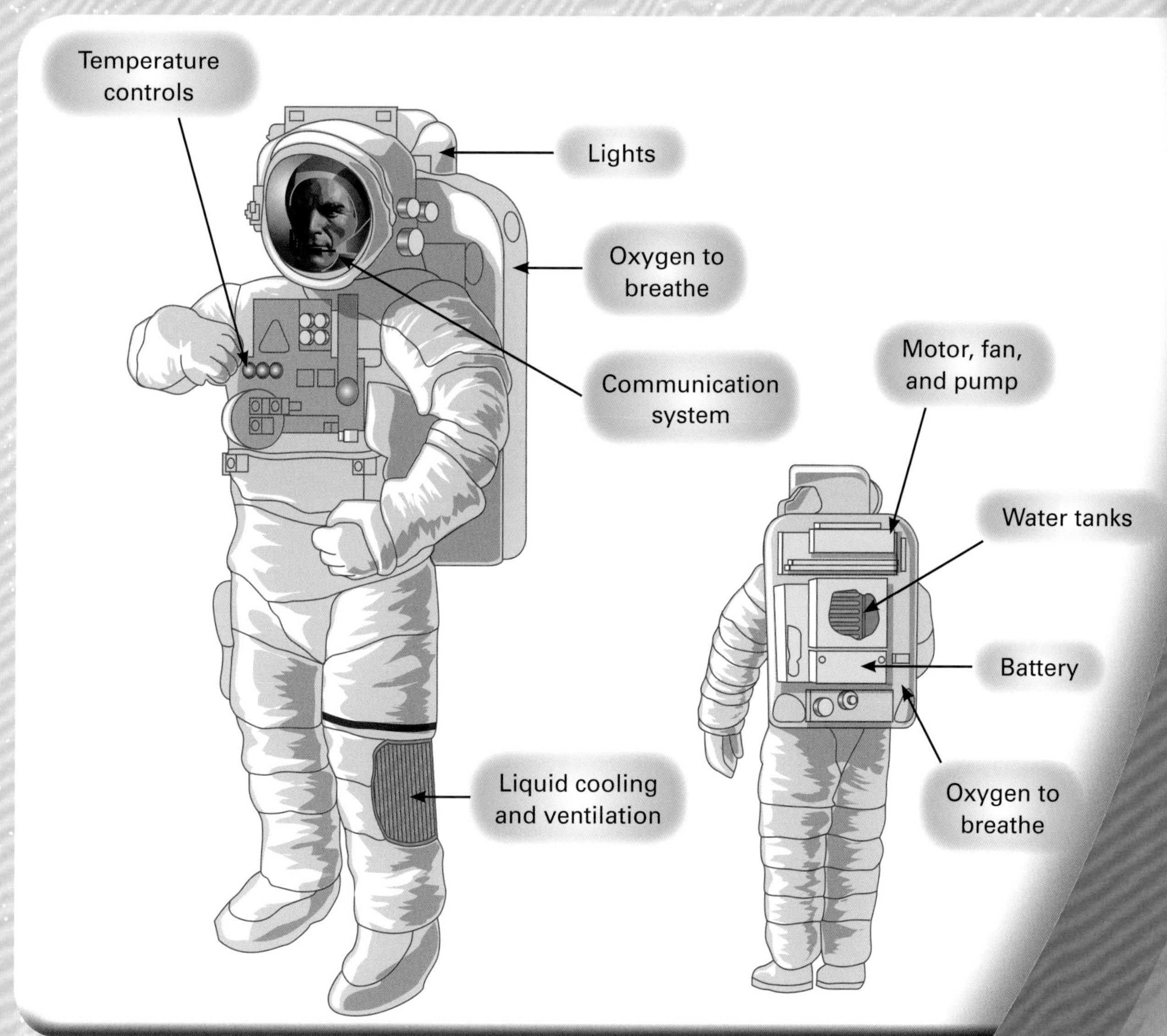

Does the Moon Move?

The Moon moves in two main ways. It orbits Earth, and at the same time it rotates on its axis.

The Moon Orbits Earth

The Moon is a satellite of Earth, which means it orbits Earth. It does this because Earth's gravity pulls on the Moon as it moves through space. The Earth's gravitational pull keeps the Moon on the same orbital path and stops it from flying off into space.

It takes 27.3 days for the Moon to orbit Earth, and 27.3 days for the Moon to rotate on its axis.

FAMOUS SKY WATCHERS

In 1687, British scientist and sky watcher Sir Isaac Newton put forward his theories of motion and gravity in his book the *Mathematical Principles of Natural Philosophy*. These theories explain why the Moon orbits the Earth.

The Moon Rotates

As the Moon orbits Earth, it also rotates on its own axis. This means that it turns around like a spinning top. The Moon rotates in a counter-clockwise direction.

We Cannot See the Far Side of the Moon

The far side of the Moon is the part we cannot see from Earth. As the Moon orbits Earth, the Moon and Earth are also both rotating. Because the Moon takes the same time to rotate on its axis as it does to orbit Earth, the same side of the Moon always faces Earth. The far side is therefore always hidden from view.

Moon Fact

The Moon travels through space at 2,289 mi. (3,683 km) per hour. This is as fast as the fastest jet plane can travel in the skies around Earth.

V The first photos of the far side of the Moon were taken in 1959 by the spacecraft *Luna 3.* This photo was taken by *Apollo 15* in 1971.

How Does the Moon Affect Earth?

From Earth, the Moon looks beautiful in the night sky. However, it is more than just a pretty object. The Moon affects all living things on Earth as well as their daily lives. Scientists believe that life on Earth would be very different without a Moon.

The Moon is important to Earth in many ways.

Moon Fact

For centuries it was believed that the full moon had the power to affect people's behavior. However, modern studies have shown that this is not true.

The Moon Makes Our Days Longer

While Earth's gravity keeps the Moon in orbit, the Moon's gravity also pulls on Earth. The Moon's gravity affects Earth's **rotation** by slowing it down. Billions of years ago, Earth rotated very quickly and days were only six hours long. Since the Moon was formed, its gravity has worked to slow Earth's spin. A day is now twenty-four hours long.

What If There Were No Moon?

Without a Moon, Earth would spin more quickly and less steadily. Days and nights would be shorter, and there would be very strong winds and uneven temperatures.

V With shorter days and less even temperatures, it is unlikely that human life would have developed on Earth.

The Moon Creates Tides

The Moon's gravity affects the water on Earth. Its gravitational pull makes oceans all around Earth rise and fall twice a day. When they rise, it is known as high tide. When they fall, it is known as low tide.

Moon Fact

Each day, the times of high and low tides on any particular spot on Earth are 50 minutes later than the day before. This is because the Moon takes 24 hours and 50 minutes to travel completely around the Earth.

V High tide is followed by low tide, just over six hours later. There are two high tides and two low tides daily.

How the Moon Creates Tides

As Earth travels around the Sun, it rotates. On the side of Earth that is facing the Moon, the Moon's gravity pulls the Earth's seas and oceans toward it. This creates a high tide. On the side of the world that is not facing the Moon, the water is not pulled by the Moon's gravity. This makes it flow away from the Moon, also creating a high tide. At the same time, the parts of Earth that are not in line with the Moon have low tide. This is because these areas are not as strongly affected by the Moon's gravity.

The tides rise and fall twice a day at different times all around the world.

Life Without the Moon?

Without the Moon, there would be little difference between low and high tides on Earth. Plants and animals that have adapted to live with changing water levels would not survive.

FAMOUS SKY WATCHERS

As long ago as 150 BCE, the Babylonian astronomer Seleucus of Seleucia observed that the Moon seemed to affect Earth's tides. He noticed that tides were higher when the Moon was closer to the Sun.

The Moon Helps Us Keep Time

Before there were clocks and calendars, the phases of the Moon helped people keep track of time. One month is about the length of time that it takes the Moon to go through all of its phases. The word "month" comes from the word "Moon."

The last day on our calendar is New Year's Eve. It is celebrated around the world on December 31 every year.

Moon Fact

People in China, as well as religious Jews and Muslims all use the lunar calendar rather than the solar calendar to mark their years. Their special days do not occur at a fixed time, but instead depend on the phases of the Moon.

Keeping Time Without the Moon

If there were no Moon, months would not exist because there would be no moon phases. Time would only be marked by day and night, and the seasons.

The Moon Helps Animals To See at Night

Some animals sleep during the day, and are awake at night. These animals are nocturnal. Many nocturnal animals have developed vision that allows them to see in the low light reflected by the Moon. Nocturnal hunters tend to become busier when the Moon is full. Other nocturnal animals avoid the moonlight so they will not be hunted and killed.

What if There Were No Moon?

Without a Moon, many animals would not have become nocturnal. This could have meant that fewer types of animals would have existed on Earth.

The barn owl's eyesight has adapted to work in the low light of the Moon so that it can see its prey.

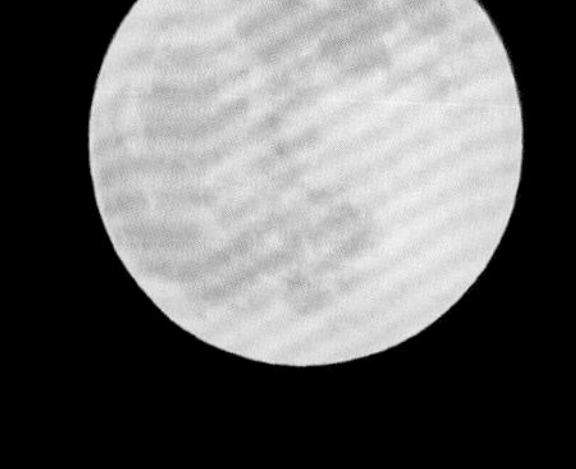

What Is the Future of the Moon?

People watching the Moon have worried that it might somehow be destroyed or one day leave Earth's orbit. However, scientists believe that although the Moon is slowly moving farther away from Earth, there are no threats to it in the near future.

Meteoroid Impacts Threaten the Moon

Although there are still meteoroid impacts on the Moon almost every day, there has not been a very large impact for millions of years. Scientists do not believe there will be another large impact in the near future. This is because there are no longer as many large meteoroids as there were when the solar system was first formed.

Famous Sky Watchers

Until 1990, the United States and Russia were the only countries to send spacecraft the Moon. Now Japan, China, and India have all sent spacecraft. The United States and China both hope to build lunar bases in the 2020s.

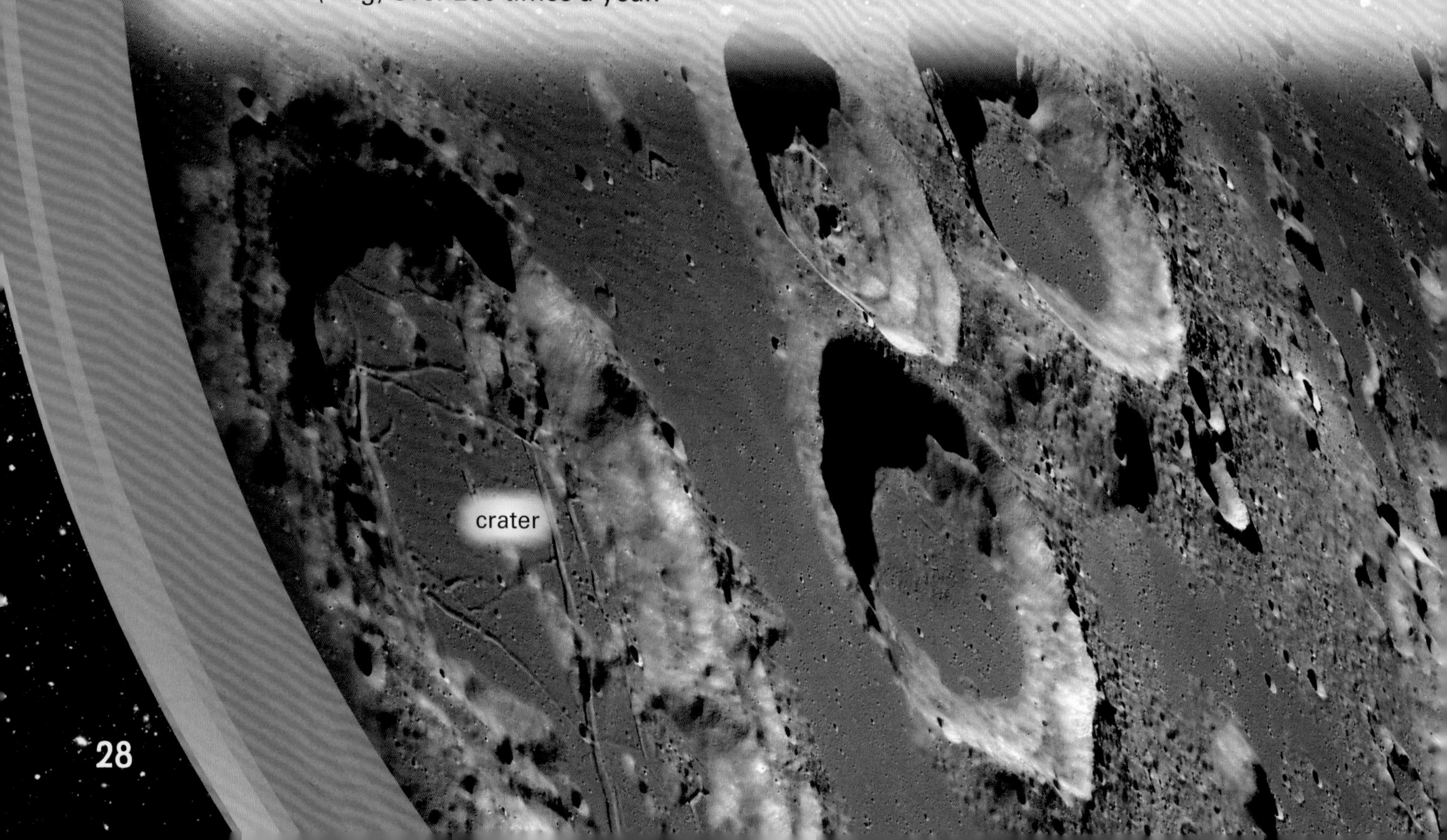

Lunar scientists think that the Moon is struck by meteoroids weighing more than 2.2 lb. (1 kg) over 260 times a year.

The Moon Is Moving Away from Earth

Scientists have discovered that the Moon is gradually traveling away from Earth. Each year it moves about 1.2 inches (3 centimeters) farther away. It is unlikely that the Moon will ever leave Earth's orbit. However, in millions of years it will look much smaller in the night sky than it does today.

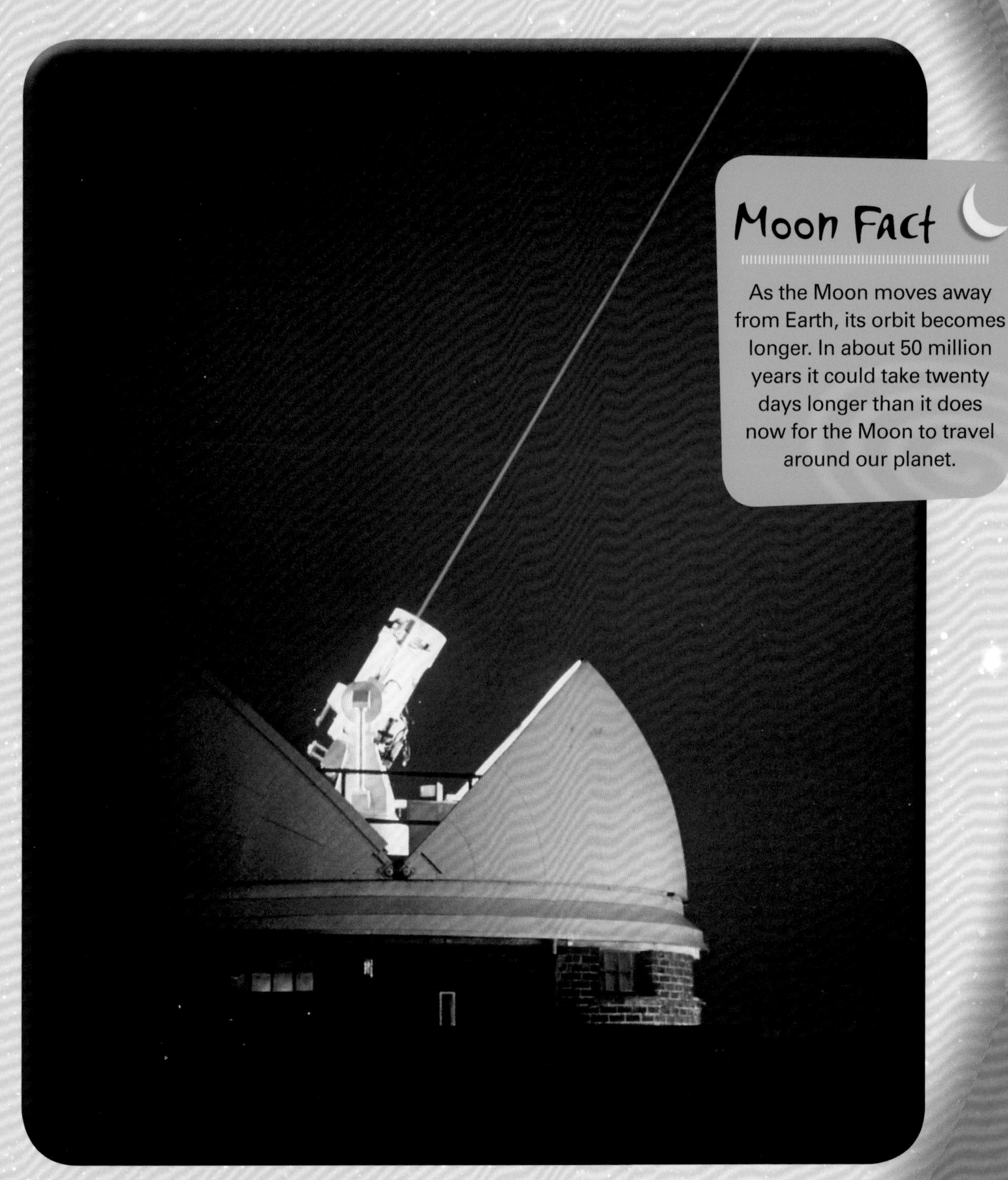

Moon Fact

As the Moon moves away from Earth, its orbit becomes longer. In about 50 million years it could take twenty days longer than it does now for the Moon to travel around our planet.

Scientists use laser beams to measure the exact distance between Earth and the Moon.

What Are the Best Ways to Moon-Watch?

Because the Moon is so close to Earth, it can be viewed with just the human eye. However, thanks to telescopes and photos taken from space, we also have other ways of looking at the Moon.

Moon Watching with the Human Eye

Look at the Moon every night for a month and see how it changes shape. Make drawings to show these different phases of the Moon.

Moon Watching through a Telescope

Watch the phases of the Moon through a telescope or **binoculars**. Do they look different from what you see with your eyes?

Moon Watching Online

Research the phases of the Moon online. What more can you learn from these websites?

Useful Equipment for Backyard Astronomy	
Equipment	**What It Is Used for**
Binoculars or a Telescope	A pair of binoculars or a telescope will help you see the craters on the Moon in more detail. They will also help you distinguish between the plains and highlands.
Map of the Moon	A map of the Moon will help you identify the features of the Moon that you can see.

Useful Websites

Apollo 11 – First Footprint on the Moon: www.nasa.gov/audience/forstudents/k-4/home/F_Apollo_11.html

BioEd Online: www.bioedonline.org/news/news.cfm?art=2766

Images for the Classroom – Earth's Moon and the Apollo Program: http://spaceplace.nasa.gov/en/educators/teachers_moon_images.shtml

Spacekids: www.spacekids.co.uk/spacesuits

GLOSSARY

asteroids Small, rocky, or metal space objects that orbit the Sun.

astronauts People who travel into space.

astronomers People who study stars, planets, and other bodies in space.

atmosphere The layer of gases that surrounds a planet, moon, or star.

axis An imaginary line through the middle of an object, from top to bottom.

binoculars An instrument with two eye pieces, for making faraway objects look bigger.

comets Small, rocky, and icy space objects that have long, shining tails that are visible when orbiting near the Sun.

extreme The highest or lowest degree of something.

gravitational pull The forces of gravity that attract two objects toward each other.

gravity The force that attracts all objects toward each other.

highlands Land that is hilly and higher than seas or plains, but is not as high as mountains.

lava Hot, liquid rock that flows out of volcanoes.

meteorites Pieces of meteoroids that have landed on the surface of larger space objects.

meteoroids Small space objects that are made of rock and metal, ranging from several feet wide to the size of a pea.

molten The process of turning solid material into a liquid form by using extreme heat.

orbits When one space object travels around another, larger space object.

phases The different stages in a cycle or process of change.

plains Low-lying, flat areas of land.

rotates Turns or spins around a fixed point or an axis, like a spinning top.

rotation The process of turning around a fixed point or an axis.

satellite A natural or human-made object that orbits a planet.

solar system The Sun and everything that orbits it, including planets and other space objects.

sound waves Moving waves in the air that produce and carry sound.

space The area in which the solar system, stars, and galaxies exist, also known as the universe.

telescope An instrument with a single eye piece, for making faraway objects look bigger.

INDEX